Everything is Under Control

Sadia Salim

BookLeaf Publishing

Presentation by *BookLeaf Publishing*

Web: www.bookleafpub.com

E-mail: info@bookleafpub.com

ISBN: 9789357442954

First edition 2023

To my friends who are constantly complaining about their sleepless lives with me. Thank you for making me feel more stable than I actually am.

I Want to Grow Up

The child says "I want to be a grown up too"
Looking at the happy woman who has no clue
That she has just influenced another.
She'll regret it when she's hungover.

What will she tell that child later on?
When he finally grows to realise she's a con,
That her life was far from jolly,
As she read her never ending list while pushing
the trolley.

She too, wanted to become an adult,
It's a collective thing, which later becomes an
insult.

Now they wish to return to their curious times,
Where they'd listen to the chimes,
Of the lunch bell
To bring them back to their silly idea of hell.
Where the hardest thing was to stop playing,
Without the constant need for worrying
About when the next pay-check will be
Because children can have things for free.

Grabbing at their pen and paper
During their hours of labour
The two wrote
Without a thought:

"I want to be happy.
I want to be child-me."

The Little Adultings

"Beep. Next customer please!"
He was sleep deprived
A normal thing for an adult beginner
His notebook sat on the counter,
Empty as ever,
"One pound, forty-nine for this."
He smiled at the customer,
Another barely awake survivor
Of the pitiful adult curse.
The two share an understanding,
Unknown to those of their surroundings.
Calculating their free time during their busy
hours,
Counting their groceries -
all of a sudden they wished they took their math
classes seriously.
But these individual problems weren't worth
their limited time,
And so they turned back to their schedules.
Because that's what adults do.
So the notebook stayed empty,
And they went on, counting their hours,
Since that was what they were taught to do.

"Beep. Have a wonderful night."

Decide Already!

Sitting behind the illuminated screen,
Her blue-light glasses became tired with her.
Biting at her thumb,
A foot hopping irresponsibly,
She had to choose something,
Something that'll mark her path in the world.
But what if she wanted to change it later on?
What if ten years from now, she realises that it
was all wrong!
"Choose already!" Her dad was frustrated,
Why does he get to be frustrated?
"It's my choice!"
But what exactly was her choice?
The arrow danced up and down.
"This one! No but this one seems the better
choice."
"This wasn't so hard for me. You're
overthinking it."
What would he know. He's an adult.
This was her future she had to think of.
Her first step towards the doors of the next stage
in life -
It was already going terrible.
"Dad! I don't know what to choose!"
"Do what your heart wants!"

How could she explain to him that her heart was
still confused.
She was still at that age,
Rational thinking was another thing she was
forcing herself to learn.
This was the worst age for decision-making.
"If you can't choose at the age of sixteen then
how will you survive?"
The arrow began to narrow down to one option.
"This'll be it then."

But what if it isn't? Ten years from today
This may be her only pathway.
What'll she say?
If her twenty six year old self decay
From her teenage decision in May?

The Great Birthday Depression

Today's weather chose to be grey,
Holiday season had begun with a wonderful
start.
Early morning and not a single thing seemed out
of the ordinary,

Going out was no longer an option as the rainfall
increased.
Reading a book felt like a hassle,
Eating the cake felt lonely.
An empty feeling grew,
Today was a day where something was supposed
to happen.

But maybe it was just a thought,
In all honesty, with the
Radio buffering to a halt,
Today was just another ordinary day.
Half eaten sandwiches,
Daily newspapers left on the tea table,
And the TV playing a music video.
Yes, everything here was ordinary.

"Do no steal" written over juice boxes,
Egg shells left on the counter,
Pots and pans all over the stove,
Radiator heat was suffocating,
Everything was left the way it was last night.
Silently pulling on the rubber gloves,
Slowly filling up the bin bag and
In that moment of cleaning, the realisation came.
Oh! That's what was missing for today.
Nobody said "Happy birthday"

The Seasonal Flu

Did you hear the breeze of that lovely spring
morning?
Or did you choose to curse it,
While you rushed your forgotten homework
outside
At the bus stop with other frantic people.

Did you dance around on the sand?
At the beach in the summer evening of a holiday
Tuesday?
Or did you cry in your room,
Because the heat of it all became too much.

How about the crunch of the leaves?
When autumn welcomes in a sense of
tranquility?
Or do you reach the trees too late,
When the rain passes by mid October.

Winter in London.
At least nothing can go wrong with that, right?
Unless… you hate the aftermath of fallen snow,
Having to slip and slide during a school day.

Oh look… snow is falling.
Unless you're reading this when the blossom
petals are floating.
Or perhaps you're watching a pair of butterflies
circle a tree.
Are we watching the same grey skies?

Do you remember how child-you would've
behaved?
Or is that just another thing you'd rather forget,
Like the four seasons you have many criticisms
for.
Me too -
I've felt the same as you.

The Walk Back Home

I watched my shadow,
It danced and stretched,
It hid behind me,
Befriended a dog,
It scared a child,
Creeping towards him,
It did all of that.

Unlike me,
who walked down the streets,
Watching my steps,
Staying away from the puddles,
Groaning at the sound of a car horn,
Blaring sirens deafening me for a moment,
Just another person returning home during the
rush hours.
Tired.

My shadow was nothing like me,
But oddly enough we are both one,
With the same routine of living.
We're both returning home.

Conversations Between Friends

We face the moon,
But we're on opposite sides,
I'm watching it right now,
While you're probably walking down the road,
Unaware of its presence.

I'll be lying on my bed soon,
You'll be working at your part time job.
Your dream of opening a bakery…
How's that going?

It's been a few years since high school,
Remember those times when we'd argue under
the stairs?
Or the time your crush said something so
ridiculous
I bursted out laughing?

we were inseparable,
Best friends, soulmates even.
Who could've thought that age would change us
too.
I'm still at our birth country.

I still see those familiar faces from my
childhood.

Oh! Did you hear?
Freya's getting married next week.
Crazy right?
We all thought she'd stay heartbroken forever.
It's surprising isn't it?

I guess… like us,
Time has moved on for everyone else too.
Who knew that all those things we did
Would just stay as memories.
Do you still have those silly pictures hung up on
your wall?

I'll be going to sleep now,
It's been a tiring week after all.
Text me when you can!
I'll try and get back to you in a few days.

Old vs New

Impatience grows
Because they know that time doesn't stay still.
But they didn't think about that when they were
younger,
We are younger.

Once in their youthful bliss,
And they're giving us advice,
Something we ignore
Because they're old.

What would they know about our struggles?
We are what they've never been.
We're ignorant.
Because they've seen what we never did.

So we laugh at their worries,
Because we know more than them.
Because our generation is ours to save
And their advice is outdated.

And now we're at that age,
Where we look back at our parents.
We think back on their words,
And the things they wanted to teach us.

They were right all along
And we've wasted our youths,
Just like they did too.

The Rainbow Outside My Room

I don't feel the way I used to,

When clouds of grey cleared away,
When the first sight of the sun was seen,
I don't remember the way I'd respond,

When the phone rang with my best friend's
name,
When I'd choke on my laughter or held my
aching stomach
I don't get excited anymore,

As I see the colours streak across the blue,
Outside my bedroom window,
Which is blocked by piles of books with names I
don't remember -

I want to feel the way I would fifteen years ago,
When my eyes would widen and I'd gasp,
I'd call my parents as I'd poke on the car
window,
"Look at the rainbow! There's treasure at the
end of it."

But I'm sitting on my bed,
My phone is on the bedside table,
And I'm looking through the window,
At the rainbow from my childhood.

Not a single twitch of the lips,
Nor my urge to grab my phone to take a picture.
Because I knew there were no treasure on the
other side.
And I had no one else to share this with.

That Summer Afternoon

We are under the sun's merciless heat,
Craving for the shadow of the trees to thicken
As we drink from the bottle of warm water.

You fanned a book to your face,
Breathing out heavily from the run.
We escaped the school's clutches,
Happily feeling the grass tickle our hands.

This'll be the last summer of our teenage years.
Can you believe it?
We'll only be getting older.

And you turn to face me,
With that smile of yours making me shudder.
And you say,
"I want this to be our forever."

Never ending

To do lists,
Wish lists,
Self-improvement lists,
Life achievement lists,
And the list goes on,
And the pile of papers is getting thicker,
And not a single thing is ticked.

You scribble mindlessly,
Another thing to add to the list,
"Complete these goals."
Only to throw it into your pile of never ending
lists.
And the word list becomes nauseating.
So you sit down and stare at the pile.
Hoping it'll be one paper less, tomorrow.
But you know you'll never complete a single
thing there.
As another thing gets added to the pile.

Nothingness

I shuffle down on the bed frame,
I've done nothing but continue scrolling,
Liking a picture that did not entertain me,
Watching the end credits rolling.
I haven't been outside for a few days,
I wonder what it would feel like,
To have the breeze against my skin,
To feel the sun warm my face.
I haven't even heard the birds chirp
At five in the morning,
Nor did I hear the rain it my roof,
And I'm watching the news on the TV,
Eating the cereal that's now become soggy.
I'm staring at the lady talking,
But not a single word made sense to me,
So I got up and put the bowl in the sink,
Ran the hot water and let the steam pass by,
And I stared outside,
At the foggy scene.
But I will not be going outside today.
I'll be back on my bed.
Once again scrolling.

Limbo

Until the sun rises,
And when it falls.
Let's sit here,
On this hill,
Watching the many colours that bruise the sky,
All for this one moment.
For a blissful silence,
As the new day begins
And the old day ends.
Let's sit here and be ignorant of the world
turning.

A Little Wise Thing

Picking flowers in the garden,
Making crowns out of daffodils,
Little squeals as the crown meets the head,
Till her laughter comes to a halt,
As she feels the flowers wilt,
And the moment the ring comes undone,
She watches as they fall one by one.
But she does not cry
Because her father taught her a wonderful thing,
You see,
There are plenty more flowers in the garden,
So if this one fails,
You can find some more,
And perhaps your crown will be prettier than
before!

Maya's Story

Her parents made her believe,
Grades were what created her worth.
So she'd sit on her desk,
Day and night.
Endlessly writing till her middle finger had a
bump.

She'd walk into her classroom,
Her nickname was blister girl,
Her fingers were always covered in them.
Not a day went by without her hands being bare.

And she'd walk back home,
Her feet dragging,
Living off of the bread she brought from the
canteen.
She had a nosebleed an hour ago.

But she was smiling,
Because she had the grades she knew would
make her parents proud.
And she was glad she didn't stop,
Handing the envelope into her mother's hands.

Their reactions were empty,
An expecting nod as they handed it back,
They sent her to her room,
She was to study once more.

So she started opening her books,
She stared at the lines,
Her eyes blurring with tears,
Realisation came to her right then.
She was never special.

The I in Us

If only you could see the things I saw,
If only you could think the way I thought,
If only you could hear the things I heard,
If only you could feel the way I felt,

But we can never know any of that,
And all we have are words,
Descriptions to work by,
Force of empathy to say
"Oh I understand"
Though we never really do,
Perhaps a glimpse through the curtains,
But can you really see what's on the left
If your right eye is the only one open?

I'll never see the things you saw,
I'll never think the way you thought,
I'll never hear the things you heard
And I'll never really feel the way you felt,

We'll never know each other,
But I can try and read between the lines,
If you do the same with me.

Blissful Heartache

Saying things out of spite,
Apologising the next day,
The slow process of healing,
The moment of forgiving,
And then the moments of laughter,
Finding silly things meaningful,.

Then the sudden shift of emotions,
Returning to the harsh words,
Falling asleep in tears,
Waking up numb.
Feeling the words of regret wash in.

And that is how life is,
And that is how it'll go.
As bittersweet as it can go.

The Familiar Becomes Distant

You notice the child smiling back at you from
the photos,
The ones your mum proudly put up on the walls,
"It's been a while, how have you been?"
The long video calls have been shorter now,
You don't have the same smile now,
You don't even remember who the child is,
"Work is tiring, Mama."
You complain, she listens,
She walks around the living room,
There isn't a single photo of the older you,
You focus on your mum,
Wrinkles formed on the middle of her brows,
Her smile lines are a lot more prominent than the
last time you saw her,
A long time passed since then.
"Mama?"
The line wavers and you disconnect.
"It's for the best."
You take this as a chance to sleep,
This'll be the way life goes,
Till the next call happens a month later.

www.ingramcontent.com/pod-product-compliance
Lightning Source LLC
LaVergne TN
LVHW021348200726

843509LV00014B/2731